The Senses

TOUCH

Angela Royston

Chrysalis Children's Books

First published in the UK in 2005 by
Chrysalis Children's Books,
An imprint of Chrysalis Books Group Plc,
The Chrysalis Building, Bramley Road,
London W10 6SP

ISBN 1 84458 167 5

British Library Cataloguing in Publication Data
for this book is available from the British Library.

Editorial Manager *Joyce Bentley*
Senior Editor *Rasha Elsaeed*
Editorial Assistant *Camilla Lloyd*

Produced by Bender Richardson White
Project Editor *Lionel Bender*
Designer *Ben White*
Production *Kim Richardson*
Picture Researcher *Cathy Stastny*
Cover Make-up *Mike Pilley, Radius*

Printed in China

10 9 8 7 6 5 4 3 2 1

Words in **bold** can be found in New words on page 31.

Typography *Natascha Frensch*
Read Regular, READ SMALLCAPS and Read Space; European Community Design Registration 2003
and Copyright © Natascha Frensch 2001-2004 Read Medium, **Read Black** and *Read Slanted*
Copyright © Natascha Frensch 2003-2004

READ™ is a revolutionary new typeface that will enchance children's understanding through clear, easily
recognisable character shapes. With its evenly spaced and carefully designed characters, READ™ will help
children at all stages to improve their literacy skills, and is ideal for young readers, reluctant readers and
especially children with dyslexia.

Picture credits

Cover: Steve Gorton. Inside: Bubbles: pages 4 (Geoff du Feu), 8 (Ian West), 9 (Loisjoy Thurstun), 10 (Loisjoy Thurstun), 12
(Jennie Woodcock), 15 (Lucy Tizard), 16 (Lucy Tizard), 17 (Ian West), 18 (Loisjoy Thurstun), 21 (Jennie Woodcock), 23
(Lucy Tizard), 25 (Catchlight), 26 (Loisjoy Thurstun), 27 (Jennie Woodcock), 28 (Lucy Tizard). Corbis Images Inc: page 6 (Guy
Stubbs/Gallo Images). Educationphotos.co.uk/Walmsley: pages 19, 22, 24, 29. Steve Gorton: pages 1, 2, 5, 7, 11, 13, 14, 20.

Contents

What is touch?

Touch is the **sense** that tells you what size, shape and kind an object is just by feeling it.

Touch also tells you when an object brushes against you or comes in contact with your skin.

Skin and touch

Your skin and brain work together to give you your sense of touch.

Everyone's skin has many fine hairs and **nerve endings** that detect touch.

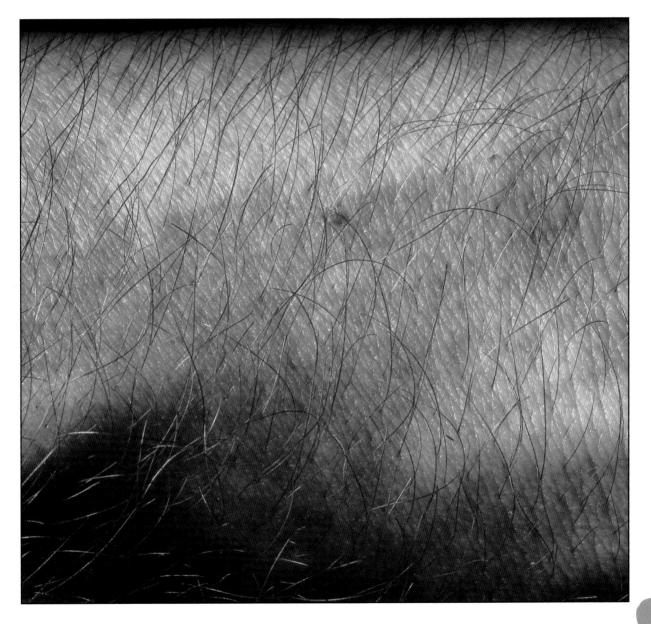

Feeling it

You usually use your hands to feel things. Stroking a pet uses a light touch.

Your fingers can tell you how different things feel. A spoon is hard. Flour is soft and **powdery**.

Rough or smooth?

Your sense of touch tells you how rough or smooth something is.

Sandpaper is rough but a pane of glass is smooth.

Sticky or slippery?

If you get jam, honey or glue on your fingers, your skin feels very sticky.

Wet soap is so slippery, it is sometimes hard to keep hold of it!

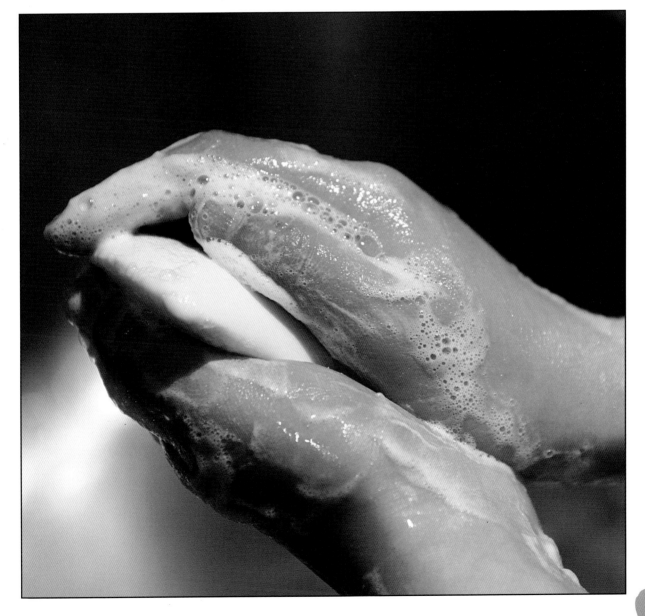

Hard or soft?

Things that are hard do not **squash** or give when you touch them.

Soft things are gentle to touch.
They can be squashed and
crumpled easily.

Hot or cold?

Your skin has nerve endings that also detect when something hot or cold touches it.

Bathing is fun if the water is not too hot or too cold. In winter, you wrap up to keep warm.

Lips and tongue

Your lips and tongue are very good at detecting when things are very hot or cold.

Test hot things with your lips or tongue. That way you won't burn your mouth.

Sharp or spiky?

Everyday objects may have a sharp point or edge. They can **pierce** or cut your skin.

Use scissors with blunt ends. If they slip, they will not cut you.

Wet or dry?

You use your sense of touch to tell if something is wet or dry.

Wet things stick to your skin, but dry things do not.

Touch and pain

A touch too hard or unexpected is painful. Nerve endings in your skin make you feel pain.

Pain warns you that something is wrong. Pain makes you rest until the **injury** is better.

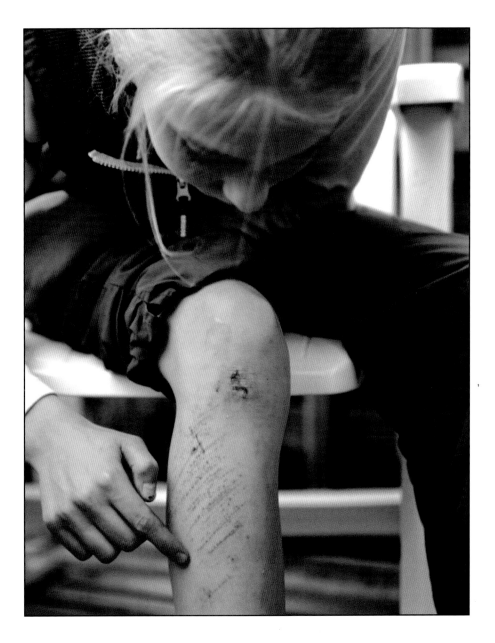

Careful touch

Some things that touch your skin may give you a **rash**. The rash may feel itchy.

Too much sunbathing can burn your skin. Putting on sunblock cream stops this.

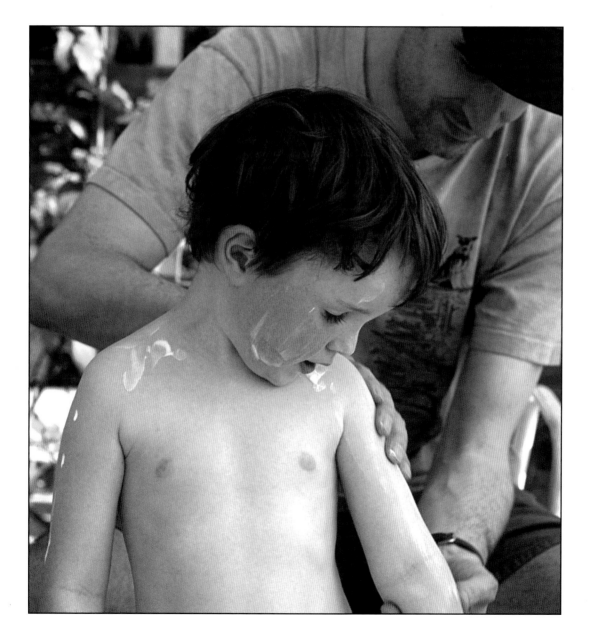

Using touch

If you cannot see, using your sense of touch is the best way to find your way around.

Blind people use touch to read. The words are printed in a pattern of bumpy dots.

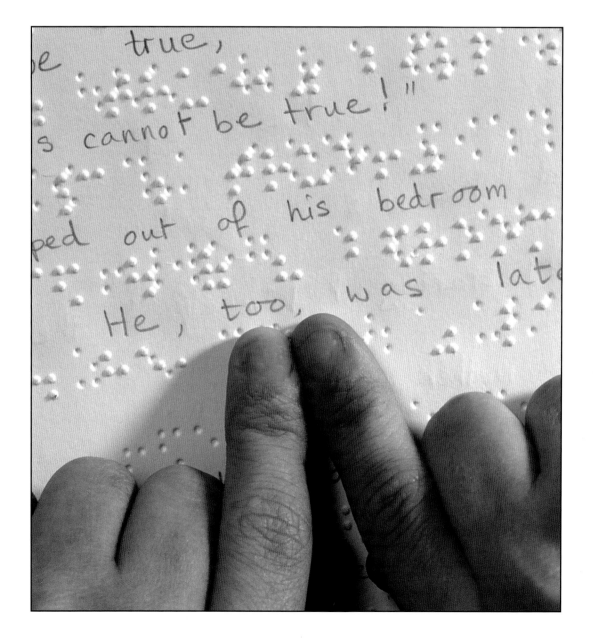

Quiz

1 What do you use to feel with?

2 Is sandpaper rough or smooth?

3 Is wet soap sticky or slippery?

4 Is a rock hard or soft?

5 Why should you test hot food and drinks with your lips or tongue?

6 Why is pain useful?

7 How can you stop the sun burning your skin?

8 How do blind people read?

The answers are all in this book!

New words

crumpled crushed.

injury damage to the body.

nerve endings parts of the body that react to particular things, such as things you touch.

pierce make a hole in.

powdery like dust.

rash many small red spots on the skin.

sandpaper rough paper that is rubbed over wood and other things to make them smooth.

sense the way you find out about your surroundings. You have five senses – sight, hearing, smell, taste and touch.

squash press to make something thinner or smaller.

Index